CW00730748

MASTER YOUR MONEY

Be a CLEVER SPENDER

Izzi Howell
illustrated by Yekyung Kwon

FRANKLIN WATTS
LONDON•SYDNEY

Franklin Watts
First published in Great Britain in 2023 by Hodder & Stoughton
Copyright © Hodder & Stoughton, 2023

Produced for Franklin Watts by
White-Thomson Publishing Ltd
www.wtpub.co.uk

Editor: Izzi Howell
Designer: Clare Nicholas

HB ISBN: 978 1 4451 8611 5
PB ISBN: 978 1 4451 8610 8

MIX
Paper from
responsible sources
FSC® C104740

Franklin Watts
An imprint of
Hachette Children's Group
Part of Hodder & Stoughton
Carmelite House
50 Victoria Embankment
London EC4Y 0DZ

An Hachette UK Company
www.hachettechildrens.co.uk

Printed in China

Words in **bold** appear in the glossary on page 30.

CONTENTS

SENSIBLE SPENDING

Whether you're on a tight **budget** or have cash to splash, it's important to spend your money wisely. This book will teach you how to be a clever spender. Read on to find out how to get the most out of your piggy bank!

Spending limit

Clever spenders work out a budget before they hit the shops. Borrowing money from other people can be helpful sometimes, but it's not a good idea to regularly spend money you don't actually have.

That pile is to spend and that pile is to save!

On the list

Shopping can be a lot of fun, but buying things you don't need is bad for your wallet and the planet. Clever spenders make a shopping list and only buy things they really want and need.

Do your research

Clever spenders look around before they shop. You can save lots of money by choosing another **brand**, buying from another shop or online, or by waiting for a special offer.

SALE

MONEY MISSION

If you get pocket money, spend it as you normally would for a month, keeping track of what you buy and where. Then, follow the advice in this book for a month, also keeping track of your spending. Compare the two months. How much were you able to save by being a clever spender?

PLAN AHEAD

One of the best ways to watch your spending is to make a plan. It's easier to make good spending choices when you've thought about how much money you have to spend and what you actually want.

Add it up

First, how much money do you already have? This could be pocket money, money from a birthday, or money earned by doing chores around the house. Add it all up to work out the total!

Pay it back

Next, think about anything you've already agreed to spend your money on. For example, you might have borrowed money from a friend and need to pay them back. Subtract this amount from your total. The amount left is how much you have to spend!

This is for you!

Get focused

It's easy to get distracted in shops and on websites and buy things you don't really want or need. A good solution is to make a shopping list. Think about how much you have to spend, what you want and how much it costs. Find out more on pages 8–9.

MONEY MISSION

If the items on your shopping list cost more than the amount of money you have to spend at the moment, make a wish list for the future! Next time you go shopping, check your wish list and see what you can afford.

LOOK AT LISTS

Your wish list will probably look quite different to your friends' because everybody has different likes and interests. But, whatever you're into, you can still make clever decisions about what to buy.

Imagine you received £40 for your birthday. Here is your wish list. What would be the best things to spend your money on?

Shirt from my favourite basketball team - £40

New book from my favourite series - £7

Going to the cinema with my friend - £6

Credit for an online game - £10

Fast fashion t-shirt - £3

This **purchase** would use up all of your birthday money. Think about how often you'd wear the shirt. Is it worth it or would it be better to use the money in another way?

If you're certain you want the shirt, why not save up for it? Use some birthday money to start your savings and then add to it with pocket money or money you've earned each week or month. This way, you won't use up all your money in one go.

This purchase doesn't use up all of your money and will give you hours of reading fun.

Spending money on experiences (see pages 26–27) can be a good **investment**. You'll enjoy the film, time with your friend and still have some money left over!

If you really enjoy the game and the credit will make it even more fun to play, this might be worth it. But once the credit is gone, it's gone! Is the extra fun worth the cost?

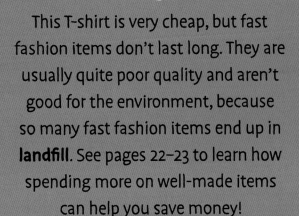

This T-shirt is very cheap, but fast fashion items don't last long. They are usually quite poor quality and aren't good for the environment, because so many fast fashion items end up in **landfill**. See pages 22–23 to learn how spending more on well-made items can help you save money!

WHAT *NOT* TO BUY

Watch out! There are a few things that should always be avoided. Take note and save your money for something better.

Quick purchase

An impulse buy is something you suddenly decide to buy without thinking it through. Often these purchases tend to be items that you don't really want or need. Advertising, special offers and sales make impulse buys more likely. To avoid impulse buys, make a list and stick to it!

2 for 1

The latest thing

It's easy to feel left out when lots of other people are buying something new and exciting. This can create pressure to buy it too, even if you won't really enjoy it. Try to ignore those feelings, and stick to things that you really want and need.

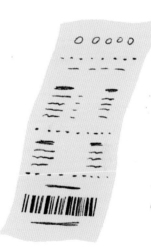

Keep the receipt!

Even if you love something at the time, don't throw away the receipt. That way, you can return or **exchange** it if you change your mind before you use it. Just make sure you leave the tags on! Normally, you can use the receipt to return or exchange the item if it breaks later on, too.

MONEY MISSION

Think back through your recent purchases. How do they make you feel now? Is there anything that you wish you hadn't bought? Try to remember what made you decide to buy it. What could you change to avoid making the same mistake again?

IN THE MOOD

Your emotions can have a big impact on your spending. Watch out for feelings that can lead to silly purchases, and get into the right mindset to be a clever spender.

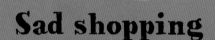

Sad shopping

If you're having a bad day, buying something to cheer yourself up can seem like a good idea. However, you might end up feeling worse if you get something you later regret! Why not brighten your day for free by chatting with a friend?

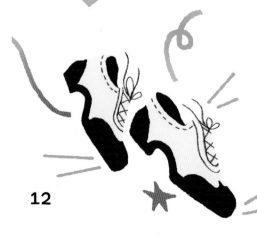

Too much excitement?

It's also risky to go shopping when you're feeling excited! Your brain is full of so much energy that it can't think things through clearly. On those days, stay away from the shops or shopping websites and express your excitement by playing, dancing or taking a walk.

Before you buy

If you're heading to the shops, get ready in advance. Work out your budget and list (see pages 6–9) at a calm time. Try to sleep well the night before so you're well rested and in a happy mood.

Take care

A little bit of preparation can make sure you stay in a good mood at the shops. Bring a snack and some water, and take a break to sit down and recharge. If you aren't enjoying yourself, leave! You can always come back another day.

IGNORE THE ADVERTS

Adverts are very good at persuading us that we really need something and we need it now! But there are a few ways to resist the power of advertising.

Take a break

Advertising is everywhere – on TV, on the Internet and in games, to name just a few places. Try to spend plenty of time doing advert-free activities, such as exploring outside, playing board games or reading books.

Make a list

When you do see adverts, write down a list of anything advertised that you like. Then, come back to the list a few days later. How many items do you still want? Taking a break helps you to think more clearly.

Don't believe everything

Remember that adverts aren't real! The people in adverts are actors and are being paid to say nice things about the product advertised. Just because they say that something is amazing and a must-buy doesn't mean that it's actually true.

Fake lives

Adverts are designed to make us feel unsatisfied. They show people with perfect lives and all the latest toys and clothes. This makes viewers think that they could have the same life if they bought the product being advertised, but sadly, it's not that simple!

GET THE BEST DEAL!

Once you've made the decision to buy something, the next question is where from? Taking the time to check different options can save you some extra pennies!

Shopping around

Prices can vary a lot from shop to shop, so it's worth checking to see if the item is cheaper elsewhere. Ask an adult to help you look online. Don't forget to include the cost of postage and be careful – if the price online seems too good to be true, it probably is!

This or that?

Instead of buying the same brand every time, check out different brands. You can find some great deals where the quality is the same, but the packaging and price is much lower!

16

Shop second-hand

Charity shops are filled with good quality **second-hand** clothes, books and games that cost far less than they did new. Choosing to shop second-hand is good for your wallet and the environment, as it gives unused items a new home, rather than sending them to landfill.

MONEY MISSION

Pick something from your wish list. Go to the shops with an adult or look online to see how much the items cost in different shops. Where is it cheapest? How much could you save if you bought it second-hand?

SIZE VS COST

Low prices can sometimes be misleading. Use simple maths to work out the cost per weight and see if you're actually getting a good deal!

Is bigger better?

Which of the bags of crisps below is the biggest bargain? The small bag? It is much cheaper, but you only get 20g of crisps. The large bag is more expensive, but you get loads more crisps. But which one is actually cheaper per weight?

96p

50p

80g

20g

Work it out!

To work out which bag is cheapest, you need to work out the cost per weight. Let's use 10g here.

There are 2 lots of 10g in 20g. So to work out the price per 10g, you divide the price of 50p by 2, which makes 25p. So the price per 10g is 25p.

The large bag weighs 80g. There are 8 lots of 10g in 96g, so we also need to divide the price by 8. 96p divided by 8 is 12p, so the price per 10g is 12p.

You get more for your money if you buy the bigger bag. Don't eat them all at once though!

Think it through

Sometimes you can make big savings by buying a bigger container of something you use everyday. But it won't always be possible. You might not have enough money to afford the bigger version, or space to store it. If you are only going to use a small amount, there's no point in buying extra.

BIG SAVINGS

Sales and special offers happen often, and can help you save quite a bit of money! However, you're only saving money if you buy things you need, so don't be tempted just because it's on offer.

Seasonal sales

Many shops hold sales at certain times of year. These sales are usually to get rid of seasonal items, like swimming costumes from the summer, or holiday gifts. If you're organised, you could pick up items for later in the year for half the price!

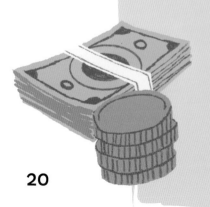

MONEY MISSION

Choose your favourite shop and note down when they hold their sales. Next year, you'll know when the sales will be so you can shop at the cheapest time of year!

On offer

If you need to make your purchase soon, keep an eye out for special offers. You might not save as much as in the big sales, but you'll be able to get your items right away!

50% OFF

Points party

Some shops offer points cards, where customers can collect points with every purchase. You can use these points to get discounts and save money! Ask an adult if they can sign up so that you can collect points together.

+5

+7

+1

+12

SPEND TO SAVE

Sometimes it pays to think about long-term savings. Cheap items are often low quality, and need replacing sooner than higher-quality, more expensive products.

Choices, choices, choices

Look at these two reusable water bottles. The plastic one is just £7.50 but it's low quality. The metal one is £12 but well made and will also keep your drinks hot or cold. If you could afford to buy either bottle, which one would be the most sensible purchase?

Gone in a flash

Buying the plastic one leaves more money for other things. But oh no! One month later, you drop your water bottle on the floor and it cracks. You now need to buy another bottle for £7.50. Four months later, the new bottle starts to leak, so you spend another £7.50 on a new one. Total spend = £22.50

Years and years

If you chose to buy the metal one, you would have less money left for other things at first. But your bottle ends up lasting several years! You spent more money upfront, but you didn't need to replace your bottle for ages. Total spend = £12

Saving the planet too!

Buying higher-quality items that last longer is also better for the environment. It reduces the amount of rubbish sent to landfill, and the amount of **resources** needed to make more stuff.

BETTER CHOICES

Some items are more expensive, but they are better for the environment and the people who produce them. Next time you're in the supermarket, take a look at the different options available.

Happy eggs

The cheapest eggs come from chickens that are kept inside small cages all day. Free-range eggs are more expensive. They come from chickens that can spend time outside. Choosing a cheaper brand of a product such as pasta can free up money in your shopping budget for more expensive items, such as free-range eggs.

Poisonous pesticides

Wild animals, including bees, are killed by the **pesticides** used on most fruit and vegetable farms. Organic fruit and vegetables, which are grown without pesticides, cost more but are better for the environment.

A fair deal

You might see 'Fairtrade' sugar, bananas or chocolate. This means that the farmers who grow and produce these products are paid a fair price, which makes Fairtrade items slightly more expensive. However, buying Fairtrade helps to reduce **poverty**.

Local choices

Buying from small, local food shops helps to support the people who live in your area. These shops tend to cost a little more, but you know that your money is going straight to the shop owner and supporting your local community.

25

EXCITING EXPERIENCES

Being a clever spender isn't just about saving money. It's also about thinking about the best way to use your money. Sometimes spending money on an experience can be much more fun than buying something.

Worth it?

Buying something new can be really fun! But then it breaks, you grow out of it or you lose interest, and the magic is gone. Maybe it wasn't such a good purchase after all ...

Double the fun

Spending money on an experience, like a trip to a theme park or a sports match, is fun while it lasts *and* fun afterwards, as you get to enjoy the special memories forever!

Picking a present

Next time it's your birthday or a holiday, think about fun experiences as well as gifts! A special trip or day out might be more fun than another toy or piece of clothing.

MONEY MISSION

Why not organise a special event as a gift to a friend or family member? It doesn't have to cost a lot of money. You could set up a movie night at home with their favourite film, or a picnic in the park with their favourite foods.

THE POWER OF MONEY

Money can make a big difference to the lives of other people. Donating to charity helps others and will make you feel good! Why not encourage your friends and family to get involved too?

Supporting the planet

Which cause is important to you? If you're interested in the environment, why not donate to a charity that protects animals and their habitats, or that helps to clean up pollution?

Helping people

Some charities support people who live in poverty, or who are suffering because of war or natural disasters. You can donate to international charities that help people in other countries or local charities that work with people in your community.

Strength in numbers

Boost your donation by organising a **fundraising** event at school. You could sell cakes, tickets to a concert or second-hand items. Decide together as a class which charity to support.

MONEY MISSION

Combine your money with that of friends and family to boost your donation! Ask everyone to donate what they can afford and suggest their favourite charity. Take a **vote** – the winning charity gets the cash!

GLOSSARY

brand – a product made by one company with its own name

budget – a plan that shows how much money someone has and how it can be spent

exchange – to take something back to the shop where you bought it and change it for something else

fast fashion – clothes that are made and sold cheaply so that people can buy new clothes often

fundraising – describes something where money is made and collected for another purpose, such as a charity

investment – spending money or time on something in order to achieve a good result in the future

landfill – a place where large amounts of rubbish is buried under the ground

pesticide – chemicals used on farms to kill insects and other small animals

poverty – being very poor

purchase – buying something

resource – a natural material that can be used to make something else, such as oil or metal

second-hand – describes something that isn't new and used to belong to someone else

vote – a way of making a decision in which everyone gets to choose their favourite option. The option chosen by the most people wins

FURTHER INFORMATION

Books

Be a Young Entrepreneur
by Adam Sutherland and Mike Gordon (Wayland, 2018)

What is Money? (Money Box)
by Ben Hubbard (Franklin Watts, 2020)

Websites

natwest.mymoneysense.com/parents/games-interactives/robot-restaurant/
Play a game to practise sticking to a budget.

www.bbc.co.uk/bitesize/topics/z8yv4wx/articles/zgghgdm
Learn more about figuring out your needs and your wants.

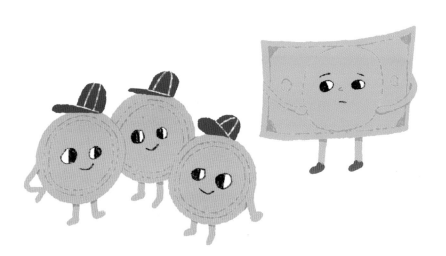

INDEX

MASTER YOUR MONEY

TITLES IN THIS SERIES

Be a CLEVER SPENDER

- Sensible spending
- Plan ahead
- Look at lists
- What not to buy
- In the mood
- Ignore the adverts
- Get the best deal!
- Size vs cost
- Spend to save
- Big savings
- Better choices
- Exciting experiences
- The power of money

Be a SUPER SAVER

- Super savings
- Starting to save
- Need or want?
- Great goals
- Tempted?
- Switch to save
- Make do
- Stay motivated
- A safe place
- Getting interest
- Keeping it safe
- Safe online
- So you've saved ...

Know YOUR MONEY

- Money, money, money
- Around the world
- Digital dollars
- Cryptocurrencies
- Making money
- Bank basics
- Loans
- Brainy borrowing
- Tax
- Rich ...
- ... and poor
- A helping hand
- The future of money

Make MEGA MONEY

- Make money!
- Get going
- Business basics
- Home help
- Take care
- Make a sale
- Excellent events
- Crafty business
- Write away
- Cook it up!
- Online artist
- Stay safe
- Made it!